11/18

Engineering
Careers

Christine Wilcox

ReferencePoint
Press®

San Diego, CA

About the Author

Christine Wilcox writes fiction and nonfiction for young adults and adults. She has worked as an editor, an instructional designer, and a writing instructor. She lives in Richmond, Virginia, with her husband, David, and her son, Anthony.

© 2019 ReferencePoint Press, Inc.
Printed in the United States

For more information, contact:
ReferencePoint Press, Inc.
PO Box 27779
San Diego, CA 92198
www.ReferencePointPress.com

Picture Credits:

Cover: gorodenkoff/iStockphoto.com
6: Maury Aaseng
20: Associated Press
29: Monty Rakusen Cultura/Newscom
46: Photos.com/Thinkstock Images
53: iStockphoto.com/franckreporter
69: iStockohoto.com/ilkercelik

LIBRARY OF CONGRESS CATALOGING-IN-PUBLICATION DATA

Name: Wilcox, Christine, author.
Title: Engineering Careers/by Christine Wilcox.
Description: San Diego, CA: ReferencePoint Press, Inc., 2019. | Series: STEM Careers series | Audience: Grade 9 to 12. | Includes bibliographical references and index.
Identifiers: LCCN 2017056181 (print) | LCCN 2017059308 (ebook) | ISBN 9781682824320 (eBook) | ISBN 9781682824313 (hardback)
Subjects: LCSH: Engineering—Vocational guidance—Juvenile literature.
Classification: LCC TA157 (ebook) | LCC TA157 .W494 2019 (print) | DDC 620.0023—dc23
LC record available at https://lccn.loc.gov/2017056181

Contents

Engineers: Master Problem Solvers

This book would not exist without engineers. Engineers designed the computer it was written on and the software that created its pages. They invented the machines that harvested trees and turned them into paper and the machines that printed the pages and bound them together. Everything on the trucks that shipped the book—from the engine to the electrical system—was designed by engineers, as were the roads, tunnels, and bridges on which the truck traveled. The school or library where the book was shelved was also designed by engineers. Reading the book in electronic form? Engineers made that possible, too.

Scientists use math and science to understand and describe the world. Engineers, on the other hand, use that knowledge to solve problems. They use scientific principles and the latest advances in technology to design complex machines, structures, and systems. Most have a natural aptitude for math and science, and all are intensely curious about how things work. They combine the critical-thinking skills of scientists with the creativity of artists. They are inventors, designers, and master problem solvers.

A Vast Field

As master problem solvers, engineers can specialize in dozens of areas. For instance, chemical engineers use chemistry to create products like medicine, plastics, fuels, and even food. Electrical engineers use the properties of electricity to design electronic devices and systems. And mechanical engineers—the most versatile discipline—design all types of machines.

However, students who graduate with a degree in one area of engineering are not restricted to a career in that area. For instance, some computer engineers have a degree in electrical engineering, and some aerospace engineers have a degree in mechanical engineering. And environmental engineers, who use engineering to tackle environmental problems, can have a degree in almost any type of engineering.

There are also quite a few career choices that are closely associated with engineering that do not require an engineering degree. Students who are looking for a more hands-on career can become surveyors, machinists, construction workers, mechanics, or engineering technicians. Engineering technicians, for example, are involved in making sure an engineer's plans are carried out correctly, and they spend a lot of time in the field running tests, taking measurements, and supervising projects. While engineers must have a bachelor's degree, technicians need only to complete a training program or obtain an associate's degree.

Not Just for Men

Traditionally, engineering has been a male-dominated field, a situation that some women have found to be challenging. In a recent *Huffington Post* article, staff writer Rebecca Adams notes that some women feel unwelcome in the field. She cites one respondent to a survey of female engineers by the University of Wisconsin: "There isn't a strong network of females in engineering. You either need to learn to be 'one of the guys' or blaze the trail yourself, which is very difficult." For this reason, Adams explains, women—including the respondent, currently leave the field in greater numbers than do men.

This situation is changing, however. Both the education system and the engineering field are working hard to change the ratio of men to women in engineering. According to the Bureau of Labor Statistics, about 20 percent of engineering school graduates are women, and that number is rising. In addition, schools are encouraging female students to pursue careers in STEM fields, and STEM companies are increasing the number of women they hire. This

Careers in Engineering

Occupation	Minimal Educational Requirement	2016 Median Pay
Aerospace engineer	Bachelor's degree	$109,650
Biomedical engineer	Bachelor's degree	$85,620
Cartographer and Photogrammetrist	Bachelor's degree	$62,750
Chemical engineer	Bachelor's degree	$98,340
Civil engineer	Bachelor's degree	$83,540
Civil engineering technician	Associate's degree	$49,980
Health and safety engineer	Bachelor's degree	$86,720
Industrial engineer	Bachelor's degree	$84,310
Landscape architect	Bachelor's degree	$63,480
Mechanical engineer	Bachelor's degree	$84,190
Surveyor	Bachelor's degree	$59,390

Source: Bureau of Labor Statistics, *Occupational Outlook Handbook*, 2017. www.bls.gov.

means that qualified women—especially those with graduate degrees in engineering—will have excellent job prospects in this field.

Internships Make a Difference

For both women and men, college internships—paid and unpaid positions that give students real-world experience in their field (sometimes for academic credit)—are extremely important to a young engineer's career. An internship often leads to a first job after graduation. It also gives students invaluable experience. As civil engineer Looly Lee explained in a March 2016 YouTube video titled *Civil Engineering: Reality vs Expectations*, "Your experience from internships or fieldwork, that's what's weighed most when getting hired." Lee works in the construction industry, and she said her education would not have been complete without internships. "You as an engineer kind of know why that concrete column would support that slab," she explained. "But seeing the connections and seeing what it really takes logistically . . . that's where your real education is."

Middle and high school internships are also extremely valuable. Not only do they give students a good idea of what engineers do, they also can help students get into a college program or get an engineering-related job after high school. Engineering internships for young people are easily searchable online. In addition, many universities have summer camp programs for high school students. And because industries are committed to encouraging students to pursue these careers, many of these opportunities are free or have scholarships available.

For students who like math and science, who are curious about how things work, and who love to figure out innovative ways to solve problems, engineering is an ideal career. Engineering degrees are also extremely versatile and can add value to almost any job. Students with degrees in engineering can go on to become lawyers, scientists, entrepreneurs, teachers, chief executive officers, or even astronauts. Regardless of where their careers take them, one thing is certain: Those who pursue a career in engineering will be uniquely qualified to make a real and tangible difference in the world.

Environmental Engineer

What Does an Environmental Engineer Do?

"Most people really don't know what environmental engineers do," says Dan Wittliff, an environmental engineer in Austin, Texas. As he explains in *U.S. News & World Report*'s online article about the best engineering jobs of 2017—of which environmental engineer was ranked number one—environmental engineers are not environmentalists. "It's not only about Earth Day and environmental consciousness," he says. "Those can be part of what an environmental engineer does, but . . . you're really focused on what the regulations say, what you're required to do to meet those regulations and how you're going to do it, [while also bearing in mind] the cost and the timeline." In other words, while environmentalists work to pass laws and regulations that protect the environment, environmental engineers come up with innovative ways for industries to adhere to those laws.

According to the environmental engineering web page for Northwestern University in Evanston, Illinois, environmental engineers address important questions like, "Is the water safe to drink? Is the air dangerous to breathe? Should we eat the fish we catch or the crops we grow? Do our living and workspaces pose special threats to our health? Environmental engineers answer these important questions every day and stand at the threshold between natural environmental systems and human societies." In other words, they use their engineering expertise to design, improve, maintain, or evaluate systems that protect people and the environment.

Environmental engineers focus on the health of the earth's air, water, and soil. They help design municipal water supply systems, industrial wastewater treatment plants, and sewer and rainwater runoff systems. They evaluate the environmental impact of construction sites and advise companies on ways to comply with environmental regulations. They work on ways to stop ozone depletion, acid rain, and global warming. They help design technology that reduces the carbon emissions created by vehicles or manufacturing plants, or they work with agricultural specialists on ways to create sustainable farming practices that do not pollute the soil and environment. They also study environmental issues, conducting research that can be used to create environmental regulations.

Entry-level environmental engineers spend a lot of their time in the field, supervising environmental engineering technicians or doing technical work themselves. They take air, soil, and water samples; they install and maintain equipment designed to detect pollution; and they interview property owners about signs of contamination. They inspect construction sites or treatment plants and write reports on whether the site is in compliance with environmental regulations. Entry-level environmental engineers working on research projects collect and map data, design models that predict the impact of pollutants, and write reports about their findings.

As environmental engineers become more experienced, they spend more time in the office designing and managing projects and supervising less experienced engineers. Some design systems or devices using computer-aided design (CAD) software. Some work on teams with scientists and other engineers on large-scale projects. Others consult with businesses, offering advice about how to obtain permits and adhere to governmental regulations. The most senior environmental engineers lead large projects, interact with clients and government officials, give presentations, or give expert testimony in environmental safety litigation cases. They may also work in research and development, creating cutting-edge technologies that keep the air, water, and soil clean and safe.

How Do You Become an Environmental Engineer?

Education

Environmental engineers must have a bachelor's degree in engineering. However, their degree does not necessarily have to be in environmental engineering. Environmental engineering is a relatively new kind of engineering that branched off from civil engineering—the engineers that build roads, bridges, reservoirs and dams, and public buildings. The discipline is also closely related to chemical engineering. In fact, almost any type of engineer can work in environmental engineering.

Students who do enroll in environmental engineering programs will take courses such as applied science (including environmental microbiology and environmental chemistry), engineering principles, math, CAD, ecology, fluid and soil mechanics, hydraulics, statistics, hazardous and solid waste management, and groundwater engineering.

Students should choose an engineering program that has been accredited by the Accreditation Board for Engineering and Technology (ABET). ABET's website has a comprehensive list of all accredited programs. This list is a good starting place for students who are deciding where to go to college.

Many environmental engineers earn a master's degree, which typically takes two years. Environmental engineers must have at least a master's degree in order to teach at a college or university or to participate in research and development. Some colleges and universities have combined undergraduate and graduate programs that allow engineers to earn both their bachelor's degree and their master's degree in five years.

Certification and Licensing

A professional engineering (PE) license is not required for environmental engineers who are starting out in their field, and many new graduates do not pursue getting their PE license until later in their careers. However, a PE license is required if an environmental engineer wishes to offer his or her services to the public, and being licensed can help with advancement. One of the requirements of a PE license is a degree from an ABET-accredited institution. Additionally, license candidates must have acquired four years of related work experience after graduation and pass a two-part exam. The first part of the exam is usually taken right after graduation.

After becoming licensed, environmental engineers can become board certified by the American Academy of Environmental Engineers and Scientists (AAEES). The AAEES offers certification in eight specialties, such as air pollution control, environmental sustainability, radiation protection engineering, and hazardous waste management and site remediation (the process of cleaning up areas contaminated with pollution or dangerous waste products).

Volunteer Work and Internships

There are few volunteer opportunities for environmental engineers, but students interested in this career should see what types of STEM programs are available in their middle or high school. Environmental engineers often collect data samples from the environment, and STEM programs or STEM summer camps can give students experience with field and laboratory science practices. Internships may also be available to high school students or recent graduates.

Internships for undergraduate students or recent graduates are an extremely important part of an environmental engineer's education, giving them real-world experience in their field. Tyler Oshiro, a junior at the University of Washington in Seattle, completed his summer internship at an engineering firm in Hawaii. "I used GIS [geographic information system] to map potential locations for satellite [water] treatment plants on Maui," he explains on the university's civil and environmental engineering web page. "[I gained] experience in pump design, database creation, underground injection control (UIC) monitoring, and even got to tour several wastewater treatment plants to see firsthand how each component operates." Internships like the one Oshiro completed can also lead to job offers, as many employers use their internship programs to recruit new hires among recent graduates.

Skills and Personality

Like all engineers, environmental engineers need to have good critical-thinking and problem-solving skills. They also need to be able to find creative solutions to the problems they face on the job. In addition, environmental engineers need good reading skills so that they can understand regulatory code, legal writing, academic writing, and other complex types of writing. They must be good communicators as well and have strong report-writing skills. Finally, because environmental engineers work on teams made up of many different types of professionals, they must have strong interpersonal skills.

On the Job

Employers

According to the Bureau of Labor Statistics (BLS), federal, state, and local governments collectively hire the most environmental engineers, followed closely by architectural and engineering firms. Another large employer is management, scientific, and technical consulting services. These three groups make up about 80 percent of all employers of environmental engineers.

California employs almost twice as many environmental engineers (7,360) as New York, the state with the second-highest level of employment (3,300). This is due, in part, to California having the strictest environmental laws in the United States. Pennsylvania, Texas, and Massachusetts rank third through fifth in employment levels, respectively.

Working Conditions

Because the work of environmental engineers is so varied, the setting in which they work depends on their specialty or the nature of the task they are involved with. Some spend most of their time in offices, while others do a lot of work in the field. Some travel frequently, especially if they work as consultants. Environmental engineering consultants often have to spend several days to several weeks at a time working remotely from home base.

Most environmental engineers work full-time on a regular schedule. Those who work on projects that are time sensitive may have to work extra hours to meet deadlines. The BLS reports only about one out of five environmental engineers worked more than forty hours a week.

Earnings

According to the BLS, in May 2016 the median salary for environmental engineers was $84,890. The lowest-paid 10 percent earned about $49,830, and the highest-paid 10 percent earned about $130,120. Of the top employers of environmental engineers, the federal government paid the highest median salary ($102,280), and state governments paid the lowest median salary ($74,730). On average, environmental engineers working on nonresidential construction projects (public or private) earned the highest average wage at $113,990.

The BLS also reports that environmental engineers employed in Alaska earn the highest average salary at $123,900. Environmental engineers in California earn the second-highest average salary at $105,160.

Opportunities for Advancement

Environmental engineers advance in their field based on their experience and professional credentials. They become team leaders, manage the work of less experienced engineers, and are given more autonomy over projects. Some move into executive positions, while others pursue master's degrees or PhDs in their area of expertise. Some environmental engineers become independent consultants or start their own environmental engineering consulting company.

What Is the Future Outlook for Environmental Engineers?

According to the BLS, jobs in environmental engineering are projected to grow by 8 percent through 2026, about as fast as average for all occupations. Students who pursue master's degrees in environmental engineering will have the best job prospects in this industry.

Recent changes in the priorities of the federal government have caused the BLS to reduce its growth projections significantly. However, the BLS notes that more environmental engineers will be needed in the future to help state and local governments address concerns in several key areas, including making sure the water supply is clean. Global warming has increased the incidence of drought, which means that localities are looking for ways to use water more efficiently. In addition, there is concern about water contamination from increases in the fracturing extraction of natural gas. More environmental engineers will be needed to help companies stay in compliance with regulations that address these concerns.

It is likely that adverse human impact on the planet will continue to affect the water, air, and soil and put human health at risk. Regardless of the political climate, environmental engineers will always be needed to protect human health and to come up with new ways to protect the environment.

Find Out More

American Academy of Environmental Engineers (AAEE)
121 Madison Ave.
New York, NY 92103
website: www.aaee.net

The AAEE is dedicated to helping students interested in pursuing a career in environmental engineering. Its website has hundreds of articles that describe what environmental engineers do, how to get an internship or prepare for a degree program, and how to get a job after graduation.

American Academy of Environmental
Engineers and Scientists (AAEES)
147 Old Solomons Island Rd., Suite 303
Annapolis, MD 21401
website: www.aaees.org

The AAEES is the organization that provides board certification to environmental engineers and scientists. Its website provides details about specialty areas in environmental engineering and the certification process and includes pages dedicated to careers and publications of interest to students.

Engineer Girl
National Academy of Engineering
500 Fifth St. NW, Room 1047
Washington, DC 20001
website: www.engineergirl.org

Engineer Girl is a website created by the National Academy of Engineering designed to encourage women and girls to pursue careers in engineering, including environmental engineering. Its website has information about what environmental engineers do and how to become one. It also has interviews and profiles on prominent female environmental engineers.

Environmental Science
website: www.environmentalscience.org

Environmental Science is a website devoted to sharing information about careers involved in protecting the environment. Its section on environmental engineering has information about degree programs for engineers and technicians, job listings, and related careers.

Biomedical Engineer

What Does a Biomedical Engineer Do?

Imagine that a hospital had a 3-D printer that could print functioning human organs ready for transplant. Or a surgeon had a smart scalpel that only cut cancerous tissue, leaving healthy tissue intact. Or an emergency room had an army of microscopic robots that could break up a blood clot that was starving a stroke victim's brain of oxygen. These amazing devices might sound like science fiction, but they are not. According to the online magazine *Today's Medical Developments*, all of these medical innovations will soon be available to doctors and hospitals around the world—thanks to the creativity of biomedical engineers.

Biomedical engineers work at the intersection of medicine, engineering, and technology. They use the principles of engineering to design solutions to biological and medical problems. They are responsible for designing countless lifesaving medical devices and methodologies. Some make

At a Glance

Biomedical Engineer

Minimum Educational Requirements
Bachelor's degree

Personal Qualities
Critical-thinking, problem-solving, and math skills; creativity; communication skills

Certification and Licensing
Optional

Working Conditions
Indoors in office and laboratory settings

Salary Range
About $51,050 to $134,620

Number of Jobs
About 21,300

Future Job Outlook
Growth of 7 percent

medical tools, instruments, and supplies. Others focus on medical machinery, like imaging machines. Still others make devices that enhance or restore the human body, like artificial hearts, pacemakers, artificial joints, and prosthetic limbs. For instance, in an April 2017 YouTube video titled *Why Biomedical Engineering?*, biomedical engineer Bisola Mutingwende demonstrated a state-of-the-art device that allows a person who has lost a hand to control a prosthesis with his or her remaining muscles. The device, which is strapped around the arm, senses muscle contractions and sends those signals to a computer, which translates them into movement and activates a motor inside a prosthetic hand. This allows the person wearing an artificial hand to control it through natural muscle movement. As Mutingwende explained to a group of prospective students of Birmingham City University in the United Kingdom, "As a biomedical engineer, you'll be working very closely with clinicians, patients, and computer scientists to solve real-life problems, working on projects from concept all the way to the manufacturing of that product. You'll be expected to combine your creativity and innovation with the latest technology to produce products that would help patients and improve their lives."

Another amazing device created by biomedical engineers is the 3-D bioprinter. Bioprinters cannot yet create human organs, but they can print living human tissue through a complex process described in a January 24, 2017, article in *Today's Medical Developments*: "The process is based on liquefying cells from either the patient or a donor in order to provide oxygen and nutrients. The cells are then deposited on a scaffold, layer by layer, based on a predetermined configuration customized to the patient. Then the bioprinted structure is incubated until it becomes viable tissue." This tissue is now used by pharmaceutical companies for product testing, but engineers are developing the technology at a fast pace. Russia has reported that it has created a functioning mouse thyroid gland with a 3-D bioprinter and says it will soon be able to do the same with a human thyroid.

Biomedical engineering is an interdisciplinary field, which means that not only must these engineers study physics, math, and engineering principles, they must also learn a great deal about the human systems involved in their biomedical specialty. For instance, biomedical engineers who design artificial hips must have in-depth knowledge of orthopedics; those who design pacemakers must understand cardiac medicine and computer technology; and those who create living tissue must have in-depth knowledge of organic chemistry and microbiology. For this reason, there are many sub-specialties within biomedical engineering, such as the following:

- Bioinstrumentation: uses electrical engineering and measurement principles to develop medical devices used to diagnose and treat diseases
- Biomechanics: uses mechanical principles and the study of motion in the human body to solve biological and medical problems
- Biomaterials: uses knowledge of organic and nonorganic materials to create devices that can be implanted within living tissue
- Systems physiology: uses engineering to understand how living organisms—from bacteria to human beings—function
- Rehabilitation engineering: uses aspects of various areas of engineering to improve the quality of life for people with physical impairments
- Neural engineering: uses computer technology, including artificial intelligence, to create ways that medical devices can enhance the function of the brain and nervous system

Biomedical engineering is a field in which people make a real difference in the lives of others. These engineers have created incredible devices and methodologies, including robots that assist doctors with delicate surgeries; eyewear that allows people who are paralyzed to control a computer with their eye movements; and inexpensive handheld diagnostic instruments, such as retinal scanners, that easily connect to smartphones. These and hundreds of other incredible innovations by biomedical engineers have the potential to completely revolutionize medical science and save countless human lives.

How Do You Become a Biomedical Engineer?

Education

Biomedical engineering undergraduate programs give students a broad background in science, engineering, and biology. They also allow students to focus on a specialty area. For instance, the bioengineering program at Johns Hopkins University requires students to take courses in organic chemistry, calculus, molecular biology, computer programing, modeling and simulations, and to apply principles of engineering to biological systems like the cardiovascular system or the nervous system. Students then choose a focus area, such as cellular and tissue engineering, imaging, or nanotechnology. Biomedical engineer David Belair suggests that students who want to excel in their careers should use their electives to do in-depth study in other areas of science and engineering, such as physiology or electrical engineering. In a May 2016 article in *Forbes* magazine, Belair suggested that students do a senior capstone project if their degree has an option for one. "Put in your maximal effort to this project," he wrote, "as it could lead to letters of reference, patents, publications, or any number of deliverables, attributes, and learned expertise that will help your early career."

Students who are primarily interested in research and development (R&D)—in other words, inventing and designing new devices and methodologies—should consider getting a master's degree. According to one recent biomedical engineering graduate, biomedical engineering is such a vast field that a bachelor's degree cannot prepare new engineers for the specialized work that goes on in R&D. As he explained on a January 2015 YouTube video, *Biomedical Engineer: Is it Worth It?*, a bachelor's in biomedical engineering is "almost a jack-of-all trades [degree] . . . and a lot of [R&D] companies, they don't really need that. They need someone . . . [who has] extensive training in this particular niche of the field." However, he noted that getting a master's degree (which typically takes two years) only increases a biomedical engineer's total salary

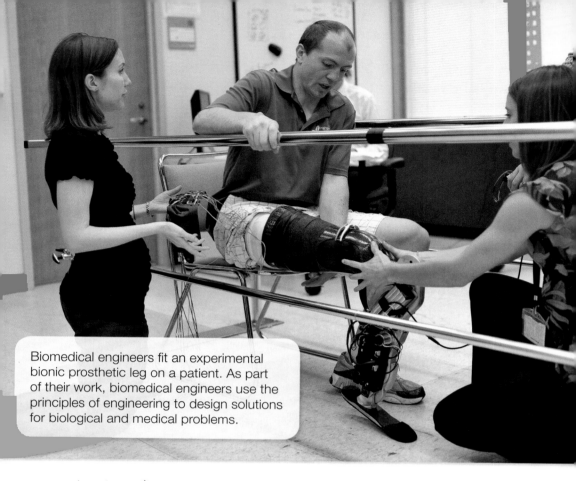

Biomedical engineers fit an experimental bionic prosthetic leg on a patient. As part of their work, biomedical engineers use the principles of engineering to design solutions for biological and medical problems.

by about $15,000 a year, on average. "I don't know if it's worth the two years and paying for school," he said. "It just depends on your passion and what you think you want to do."

Certification and Licensing

There is no formal certification available specific to biomedical engineering, and licensure is not required to work in the field. Biomedical engineers who choose to get their professional engineering license should make sure the undergraduate program they attend is accredited by the Accreditation Board for Engineering and Technology.

Volunteer Work and Internships

While there are not many volunteer opportunities in biomedical engineering, high school and college internships can be key for a successful career. These internships allow students to make contacts in the field that can lead to job opportunities. They also give students experience with research by allowing them to assist on ongoing research projects in R&D laboratories. "I cannot stress how important it is to get involved with research at an early stage," Belair wrote in *Forbes*. He encourages students to complete an internship during or after college, especially if their own undergraduate research can be part of the internship program.

Skills and Personality

Biomedical engineers must have strong critical-thinking and problem-solving skills. Creativity is also a key characteristic, especially when working in R&D. Because they work in teams, they must have strong communication skills and the ability to work with people from different scientific disciplines. Also, biomedical engineers must be good at math and have better-than-average computer skills.

On the Job

Employers

About one in five biomedical engineers work in the medical equipment and supplies manufacturing industry. These companies make surgical, medical, and dental equipment and implants. About one in six biomedical engineers work for companies that research and develop innovative medical devices, equipment, and methodologies. Biomedical engineers also work for pharmaceutical companies, colleges and universities, and health care companies.

Working Conditions

Biomedical engineers work in research laboratories and health care settings. They work in interdisciplinary teams with other engineers, health care specialists, computer programmers, and scientists. To gather data about how their devices or processes perform, they often do testing trials with human subjects. For instance, biomedical engineers developing a new type of prosthetic will spend many hours testing the prosthetic on amputees in the lab or hospital.

Biomedical engineers usually work full-time on a regular schedule. However, depending on their project, they may have to work at night or on weekends.

Earnings

The Bureau of Labor Statistics (BLS) reports that in 2016, the median salary for biomedical engineers was $85,620. The lowest-paid 10 percent of biomedical engineers earned about $51,050, and the highest-paid 10 percent earned about $134,620. Biomedical engineers who work in R&D in the physical sciences, engineering, and life science–related industries earned the most, with a median salary of $94,800. According to *U.S. News & World Report*, the highest-paid biomedical engineers work in California. For instance, the average salary in San Jose, California, is $126,430. Engineers with master's degrees or PhDs earn the highest salaries.

Opportunities for Advancement

Biomedical engineers usually advance within their fields by gaining experience. Experienced biomedical engineers often lead projects or work in a management capacity. They can also advance by creating innovative devices or methodologies and publishing their research findings in academic and industry journals. As their reputation within their field increases, they are able to work on more cutting-edge and financially lucrative projects. Some biomedical engineers are able to patent their research and start their own companies.

Biomedical engineers sometimes go to medical or dental school to increase their understanding of the biology involved in their chosen specialty, which can increase their earnings and their reputation within their field. Some go to law school and become patent attorneys. Others pursue a master of business administration degree and move into management positons.

What Is the Future Outlook for Biomedical Engineers?

According to the BLS, biomedical engineering jobs are projected to grow by about 7 percent through 2026, about as fast as average for all occupations. Technology is advancing at an exponential rate, and each new technology represents opportunities for biomedical engineers to create new types of medical devices and methodologies. In addition, as the population ages, there will be an increased demand for medical technologies that treat the diseases of aging. As Belair wrote in *Forbes*, "I don't think you'll need to worry about job placement as a biomedical engineer."

Find Out More

American Institute for Medical and Biological Engineering (AIMBE)
1400 I St. NW, Suite 235
Washington, DC 20005
website: www.aimbe.org

The AIMBE is an advocacy group for the biomedical and biological engineering professional. Its website contains an educational section that includes information for students interested in a career in biomedical engineering, as well as a section devoted to biomedical innovations.

Biomedical Engineering Society (BMES)
8201 Corporate Dr., Suite 1125
Landover, MD 20785
website: www.bmes.org

The BMES is a professional society for biological and biomedical engineers. Its website includes a career center, a blog, an electronic newsletter, links to journals, and information about student chapters of the organization.

Institute of Biomedical Engineering (IBE)
446 E. High St., Suite 10
Lexington, KY 40507
website: www.ibe.org

The IBE is a professional organization that promotes careers in biomedical engineering. Its website includes an "Ask an Expert" section, resources for students, and a career center.

Weldon School of Biomedical Engineering
Purdue University
206 S. Martin Jischke Dr.
West Lafayette, IN 47907
website: https://engineering.purdue.edu/BME

Purdue University's Weldon School of Biomedical Engineering is one of the top biomedical engineering programs in the United States. Its website contains information about biomedical engineering and its program of study, a career center, and profiles of current students.

Health and Safety Engineer

What Does a Health and Safety Engineer Do?

In 2013 an explosion erupted at a fertilizer company in West, Texas, damaging or destroying over 150 buildings—including a nearby school and nursing home. Investigators found that a fire had ignited a store of ammonium nitrate, a common agricultural fertilizer. The resulting explosion, which killed 15 people and injured more than 160, had the force of more than 7.5 tons (6.8 metric tons) of TNT. "It was like a nuclear bomb went off," Mayor Tommy Muska says in an article posted on CNN's website.

The deadly explosion caused the National Fire Protection Association to rewrite the industrial safety codes for the storage of ammonium nitrate. One of the engineers to rewrite the codes was Nancy Pearce, a fire protection engineer with over twenty-eight years' experience in the field of health and safety engineering. Because of Pearce, explosions like the one that happened in West will be much less likely to occur.

At a Glance

Health and Safety Engineer

Minimum Educational Requirements
Bachelor's degree

Personal Qualities
Critical-thinking, problem-solving, and math skills; creativity; communication and observational skills

Certification and Licensing
Optional

Working Conditions
Offices and work sites

Salary Range
About $50,580 to $134,110

Number of Jobs
About 25,900

Future Job Outlook
Growth of 9 percent

Fire protection engineers are a type of health and safety engineer. Health and safety engineers help design materials, products, machinery, or environments so they are not hazardous to people or the environment. They look at products and environments from a safety standpoint and have advanced knowledge of how people interact with machines and environments. In short, they bridge the gap between the engineers who design products or work spaces and the health and safety professionals who regulate them. For instance, health and safety engineers often work with mechanical engineers designing industrial machinery. The health and safety engineer—who often will have a degree in mechanical engineering—will make sure the machinery does not have a design flaw that may injure its operator. He or she will also design the machine's safety features required by industrial safety codes and will create safety procedures for the operator to follow.

There are dozens of specialties within the field of health and safety engineering. For instance, fire protection engineers help design equipment and buildings in order to prevent or withstand fires, make sure people can escape a structure fire quickly and safely, investigate the causes of fires, and develop materials that are resistant to fire. As Pearce explained in a March 2017 article by Luba Vangelova published on the National Science Teachers Association blog:

> My job involves much reading and research as well as traveling to conduct training sessions on how to apply the codes. My math training helps me do the necessary calculations for the codes, and my science background helps me understand the reasons behind the code requirements, such as why a chemical has a particular fire property and which materials should not be stored together for safety reasons.

Fire protection engineers also interact with the public, which Pearce enjoys. "People who have questions about the codes call me to interpret them," she told Vangelova. "For example, someone applying for a July 4 fireworks display permit may want to know at what angle to set up the fireworks and how far away spectators must be from particular types."

Other specialties within health and safety include hazardous materials management, environmental protection, product safety, and even ergonomics—a science concerned with designing workplaces and products so people can interact with them safely and efficiently. Health and safety engineers can hold many different job titles as well. For instance, engineers who make sure aircraft, missiles, and satellites function safely are called aerospace safety engineers. Engineers who investigate injuries caused by commercial products or do research to improve product safety are called product safety engineers. And engineers who design the safety processes used in fields such as health care, manufacturing, or construction are called system safety engineers. Health and safety engineers can also apply their expertise to multiple areas throughout their career. For instance, Pearce has been working as a fire protection engineer since 2012, but before that she helped get asbestos out of schools, protect health care workers from blood-borne pathogens, and develop safety procedures for workers who enter confined spaces, like tanks or manholes.

How Do You Become a Health and Safety Engineer?

Education

There are many routes to becoming a health and safety engineer, but all of them require that students earn at least a bachelor's degree. Some health and safety engineers have a degree in occupational health and safety, industrial hygiene, or environmental health and safety. These programs focus on a wide range of disciplines, such as science, public health, and management. Other health and safety engineers have degrees in one of the engineering disciplines, such as electrical, industrial, or chemical engineering, or in a more specialized area of engineering, such as fire protection engineering.

The best way for students to choose a major is to decide where their true interest lies. For instance, students who like working with machines should study mechanical engineering or a sub-specialty such as automotive, nautical, or aerospace engineering. Students who are primarily interested in health and safety may want to major in industrial hygiene or occupational safety. In addition, some degree programs combine engineering with health and safety. Large universities and universities with strong STEM programs tend to offer these types of programs.

Students should choose engineering or health and safety programs that have been accredited by the Accreditation Board for Engineering and Technology (ABET). Many certifications and licenses in the fields of engineering and health and safety require a degree from an ABET-accredited institution. ABET's website has a comprehensive list of all accredited programs. This list is a good starting place for students who are deciding where to go to college.

Some health and safety engineers go on to earn a master's degree to further specialize in their area of expertise. Master's degrees typically take two years to complete. In addition, some colleges have engineering programs that award both a bachelor's and master's degree in five years.

Certification and Licensing

It is not necessary to become a licensed engineer to work in health and safety. However, because licensed engineers (called professional engineers) are permitted to supervise other engineers and work directly with the public, many health and safety engineers get licensed later in their careers. To be licensed, health and safety engineers must have a degree from an ABET-accredited engineering program, have several years of relevant work experience, and pass two licensing exams.

Most health and safety engineers acquire professional certifications in their specialties. Certifications are available from various organizations, including the Board of Certified Safety Professionals, the American Board of Industrial Hygiene, the American Society of Safety Engineers, and the International Council on Systems Engineering. Certification can improve job prospects and help engineers advance their careers.

Volunteer Work and Internships

There are not many opportunities to volunteer in the area of health and safety engineering. However, internships in engineering or in health and safety are available to college (and occasionally high school) students at many large corporations, manufacturing and power plants, and engineering firms. The Occupational Safety and Health Administration (OSHA) lists some of these opportunities on its website. Students can also intern at regulatory agencies such as OSHA, the US Environmental Protection Agency, or the National Institute for Occupational Safety and Health.

Skills and Personality

Engineers specialize in health and safety because they have a desire to keep people and the environment safe. Many credit their job satisfaction to knowing they made a difference in people's

A health and safety engineer who specializes in aerospace evaluates the safety of an aircraft engine. These engineers help design materials, products, machinery, and environments so they are not hazardous to people or the environment.

lives. Because their jobs usually entail interacting with other engineers, safety professionals, and the public, they also tend to enjoy working with people and collaborating on teams. They should have strong communication skills and the ability to explain complex concepts and procedures to workers or other laypeople.

Health and safety engineers must have excellent critical-thinking skills and be keen observers. They must be able to spot potential safety hazards and anticipate future problems. Because their job is to solve these problems, they need to be able to use their critical-thinking skills in a creative way, finding solutions that will maximize safety while preserving productivity.

On the Job

Employers

Nearly half of all health and safety engineers are employed in the manufacturing and construction industries. Others work for the government, engineering companies, and science and technology consulting companies. In the federal government, OSHA is the largest employer of health and safety engineers. OSHA sets and enforces standards for workplace health and safety.

Working Conditions

Health and safety engineers usually work full-time, and about one in three work more than forty hours a week. They spend the majority of their time in an office environment, working with a team of specialists and technicians. Those involved with the design of safety equipment may do this work in a lab setting. Depending on their specialty, health and safety engineers may travel to construction sites, manufacturing plants, or other work sites to evaluate or test safety conditions.

Earnings

According to the Bureau of Labor Statistics (BLS), in May 2016 the median salary for health and safety engineers was $86,720, with the lowest-paid 10 percent earning about $50,580 and the highest-paid 10 percent earning about $134,110 per year. Those working for engineering services companies earned the highest median salary at $95,790. Those working for the government earned the lowest at $74,290. Additionally, the BLS reports that in 2016 the median salary for an engineering manager was $134,730, with some engineering managers earning more than $207,400 per year.

Opportunities for Advancement

Health and safety engineers can advance by gaining experience, earning certifications in their specialty, and getting a master's degree in engineering, engineering management, industrial hygiene, or a related safety field. A master's degree is usually required to move into a supervisory or management position. Engineers with advanced degrees can also develop and implement safety programs or do more complex projects independently, such as designing or modifying safety equipment.

What Is the Future Outlook for Health and Safety Engineers?

The BLS projects that employment prospects for health and safety engineers will grow by 9 percent through 2026, about as fast as average. Growth is due to an increased need in all industries to cut costs, especially those related to insurance premiums and workers' compensation. Therefore, more companies have been taking steps to reduce accidents and improve product safety. This trend will lead to an increased need for health and safety specialists of all types, including health and safety engineers. In addition, the field of software safety engineering is expected to expand in coming years, as more products and devices are controlled by computer software. Health and safety engineers who pay attention to trends in this industry and are willing to pursue continuing education and training opportunities will have the best chances for success.

Find Out More

American Industrial Hygiene Association (AIHA)
3141 Fairview Park Dr., Suite 777
Falls Church, VA 22042
website: www.aiha.org
The AIHA is a nonprofit organization that offers certification to industrial hygiene professionals, including health and safety engineers. Its website has information about the various types of certification available, as well as information for students interested in a career in health and safety.

American Society of Safety Engineers (ASSE)
520 N. Northwest Hwy.
Park Ridge, IL 60068
website: www.asse.org

The ASSE is a professional society that advocates for health and safety engineers and promotes their profession. Its website contains detailed information about practice specialties, a newsroom, and publications of interest to students.

Product Safety Engineering Society (PSES)
website: http://ewh.ieee.org/soc/pses

The PSES advances the profession of product safety engineering by encouraging innovation and collaboration within the industry. Its website contains industry news articles, a blog, and information about local chapters.

Society of Fire Protection Engineers (SFPE)
9711 Washingtonian Blvd., Suite 380
Gaithersburg, MD 20878
website: https://sfpe.site-ym.com

The SFPE is a professional society that represents fire protection engineers and advances the science and practice of fire protection. Its website has an education and careers section with information for students, such as how to prepare for a university engineering program and how to network within the SFPE.

Petroleum Engineer

What Does a Petroleum Engineer Do?

Petroleum engineers design equipment and develop plans to remove oil and gas from below the earth's surface. They are key to the oil industry's efforts to locate, extract, refine, and distribute this material safely and responsibly. Their work has a huge effect on society—from providing the energy that powers most of the world to providing the materials for thousands of petroleum-based products, such as plastics, textiles, and even medicines. "We impact hundreds of thousands of people," explained petroleum engineer Jennifer Miskimins in a February 2017 video posted on the website Energy4me. "The world runs on energy, and we provide a lot of that energy. So having that impact that you have on society makes it a lot of fun."

Petroleum engineering is a vast field; therefore, engineers typically specialize. For instance, reservoir engineers estimate the amount of oil or gas that can be recovered from an oil reservoir. They create complex computer-based models that can estimate fluid flow and pressure and determine the best method to recover oil and gas. Drilling engineers figure out how to

At a Glance

Petroleum Engineer

Minimum Educational Requirements
Bachelor's degree

Personal Qualities
Critical-thinking, problem-solving, and math skills; creativity; communication skills

Certification and Licensing
Optional

Working Conditions
Offices and work sites

Salary Range
About $73,600 to $270,000, on average

Number of Jobs
About 35,100

Future Job Outlook
Growth of 15 percent

drill a particular oil well as inexpensively and safely as possible. They are responsible for managing the people and the technology involved in a drilling operation. And production engineers develop overall processes and machinery used in oil and gas production. Other specialty areas include deepwater drilling (extracting oil from the ocean floor) and hydraulic fracturing (also known as fracking, or the extraction of natural gas from shale).

Many people go into petroleum engineering because they are attracted by the lifestyle this career can offer. Petroleum engineers often spend their careers traveling and working at job sites in foreign countries or remote, undeveloped areas. Petroleum engineers are also involved in offshore oil drilling, which means working on the ocean and specializing in the sciences that study underwater environments.

Others choose petroleum engineering because the field offers high starting salaries, as well as attractive bonuses for working in dangerous or extreme environments, such as offshore oil-drilling operations. In addition, most petroleum engineers are given more responsibility and are promoted into supervisory positions faster than engineers in other fields, which can be personally satisfying.

Historically, petroleum engineering has been a male-dominated industry, but more and more women are entering the field. Miskimins, who teaches engineering at the Colorado School of Mines, encourages young women to choose petroleum engineering because she believes women bring a unique and valuable perspective to the field. "Women's brains work differently," she said. "We look at projects differently, we look at aspects of things differently, we come at them from a different approach, and we bring a lot to this industry. And so being female in it, yeah, it might be a little tough in certain places, you might have some places that you might be the only female in that area. But you're going to make an impact."

Petroleum engineering is an exciting, lucrative, and fascinating career. As M. Christopher Doyle, a petroleum engineer with twenty years' experience working in the United Kingdom and Africa, explained, "I just fell in love. . . . It's such a cool mix of high science and high finance." Doyle, who now leads an oil and gas exploration company in Pennsylvania, told David Conti in a May

2016 article on the online news site TribLIVE that this field of engineering makes a huge difference in people's lives. "It serves a great purpose for our nation," he said.

How Do You Become a Petroleum Engineer?

Education

Petroleum engineers need at least a bachelor's degree in petroleum engineering or a related engineering discipline. Engineering programs are competitive, so students need to have good grades in math and science and should take advanced classes if possible.

Many engineers working in the petroleum industry actually earned their undergraduate degrees in another area of engineering. For instance, engineers who design the equipment used in the industry need a strong background in mechanical engineering. And engineers who specialize in protecting both workers and the environment often have a degree in either environmental or health and safety engineering. It is a good idea for students interested in working in the petroleum industry to consider where their interests lie before choosing a major.

Students who major in petroleum engineering study math, physics, chemistry, and earth sciences. Their studies focus on topics that relate to underground oil and gas deposits, such as geology, thermodynamics (the physics of heat and energy), and fluid dynamics (the physics of fluid). As Melissa Gary, a recent graduate of the petroleum engineering program at the University of Texas, told Ruth Campbell in a May 2016 article in *Odessa American* Online, "You learn a lot about the Earth and how it's composed and the mechanics of how fluid moves below the Earth—something no one thinks about. It's very intricate and extremely fascinating to me."

Some employers prefer to hire graduates who have work experience. For this reason, many petroleum engineering programs have cooperative-education programs, which allow students to earn academic credit while working in the field. In addition, because many employers prefer their engineers to have graduate degrees, it is common for petroleum engineers to have master's degrees, which typically take two years to complete. Some colleges and universities have five-year programs that award graduates both a bachelor's and a master's degree.

Certification and Licensing

Licensure and certification is not required to work as a petroleum engineer. However, because licensed engineers (known as professional engineers) are permitted to supervise other engineers and to sign off on projects, most petroleum engineers get their licenses later in their careers. To be licensed, petroleum engineers must have a degree from an engineering program accredited by the Accreditation Board for Engineering and Technology, must have about four years of relevant work experience, and must pass two licensing exams. Petroleum engineers often take the first part of their licensing exam after earning their bachelor's degrees. Passing this exam may improve one's job prospects. The second part of the licensing exam is often taken later in one's career.

Petroleum engineers can also become certified by the Society of Petroleum Engineers. Applicants must be members in the society and pass an exam. To maintain certification, they must complete sixteen hours of continuing education and professional development each year. Certification can help petroleum engineers advance their careers.

Volunteer Work and Internships

Internships are key to succeeding in the petroleum engineering industry. Internships provide invaluable educational opportunities, help students stand out to prospective employers, help with networking, and often lead to job offers. Both high school and college students should seek out summer internships. One way to find these internships is to contact the Society of Petroleum Engineers. Colleges also have career departments that connect students to summer internships.

Internships can be competitive, and many times previous internship experience will help with a current application. For this reason, the earlier students become involved in STEM activities and programs, the better. Middle and high school students interested in this career should begin building their résumé by participating in STEM programs as early as possible.

Skills and Personality

Petroleum engineers use math in their jobs every day. They must have excellent math skills and be proficient in calculus and other advanced forms of math. They also must have strong analytical and critical-thinking skills. Like all engineers, petroleum engineers use math and science to solve problems, so they must also be creative thinkers.

Nearly all petroleum engineers work in teams. They must have strong communication and interpersonal skills in order to succeed in this environment. Most also direct other workers or supervise contractors, so strong leadership skills can be extremely useful.

Finally, because many petroleum engineering jobs involve travel—and some even involve working at hazardous job sites—many people in this profession have a taste for adventure and an interest in travel and experiencing new cultures.

On the Job

Employers

Almost half of all petroleum engineers work for companies involved in oil and gas extraction. Many of these companies are based in other countries, which is one reason that so many petroleum engineers work abroad. Other employers include companies that support mining activities, companies that manufacture products from petroleum, and engineering services companies. Engineers interested in teaching and research often work at large universities.

Working Conditions

Petroleum engineers work in offices and research laboratories, but they also often have to spend long periods of time at work sites. This can entail traveling to remote locations and spending time in adverse conditions, such as on oil rigs or in very hot or very cold climates. They typically work full-time, but at a drilling site they often work rotating shifts of several days on duty followed by several days off duty.

Earnings

According to the Bureau of Labor Statistics (BLS), in May 2016 the median salary for petroleum engineers was $128,230, with the lowest-paid 10 percent earning about $73,000 and the highest-paid 10 percent earning about $208,000 per year. Those working in management earned the highest median salary at $153,320. Those working in the mining industry earned the lowest at $106,340.

The Society of Petroleum Engineers, which tracks salaries worldwide, has found that average base pay for petroleum engineers in 2016 was $143,000, but with bonuses it rose to $185,000. Engineers with up to ten years' experience earned an average of $109,000, while those with twenty-six or more years' experience earned an average of $269,740.

Opportunities for Advancement

Petroleum engineers often go through a training or internship process in their first job. As they gain knowledge and experience, they are given more responsibility and greater independence. Eventually, they lead projects or move into managerial positions. Licensure and certification help with advancement. After a decade or two in the industry, some petroleum engineers move into teaching, research, or upper management positions.

What Is the Future Outlook for Petroleum Engineers?

The BLS projects that employment prospects for petroleum engineers will grow by 15 percent through 2026, much faster than average. One of the main reasons for this growth is known in the industry as "the big crew change." As the baby boomer generation reaches retirement age over the next decade, thousands of new jobs will open up in the petroleum industry. At the same time, the petroleum industry is experiencing a great deal of growth in the area of hydraulic fracturing. Experts anticipate that there will be a skills gap that new engineering graduates will be expected to fill. To this end, the industry is ramping up its efforts to prepare high school students for careers in petroleum sciences by creating STEM academies and other special programs.

Because petroleum is a finite resource, some students may worry that a new energy source may make petroleum engineering jobs obsolete in the future. However, the American Petroleum Institute believes that petroleum will be the primary source of energy for the planet for many years to come. The institute estimates that by 2035, the number of petroleum engineers in the workplace will almost double as the industry adds about thirty thousand new positions to meet the rising energy demands of countries like China and India. For this reason, students choosing this career should have strong job prospects for many years to come.

Find Out More

American Petroleum Institute (API)
1220 L St. NW
Washington, DC 20005
website: www.api.org

The API is the national trade association for the oil and natural gas industry. Its website contains information about oil and natural gas, career information, and news about issues related to the industry.

Energy4me
website: http://energy4me.org

Energy4me is a website sponsored by the petroleum industry that educates young people about energy. The website contains information about petroleum engineer careers as well as educational articles, videos, and games.

Inside Energy

c/o Rocky Mountain PBS
1089 Bannock St.
Denver, CO 80204
website: http://insideenergy.org

Inside Energy is a news website about the energy industry created by the Corporation for Public Broadcasting. It is intended to give the public unbiased information about energy issues. Its website has dozens of articles about petroleum engineering, including information for students considering this career.

Society of Petroleum Engineers (SPE)

222 Palisades Creek Dr.
Richardson, TX 75080
website: www.spe.org

The SPE is a professional organization for petroleum engineers and those in related fields. Its website contains an energy and petroleum wiki, information about certification, and publications of interest to students.

IT Engineer

Information technology (IT) is a vast and varied industry. Within this broad discipline, IT engineers are the professionals who design computer products and systems. In general, there are three specialties within IT engineering: hardware engineers, who design physical devices and their parts; software engineers, who design the computer code that operates those devices; and systems analysts, who use existing hardware and software to design comprehensive computer systems. People in these three roles have a variety of job titles—many of which do not include the term *engineer*. However, all use the scientific principles of IT to design solutions to problems.

Hardware engineers (also known as computer engineers) design the physical objects used in computing, such as computer chips, circuit boards, memory cards, and of course, the computers themselves. In many cases their goal is to make computers faster, more powerful, and more efficient. Some hardware engineers work closely with software engineers to design devices that use computer technology, such as mobile phones and tablets. Others

At a Glance

IT Engineer

Minimum Educational Requirements
Bachelor's degree

Personal Qualities
Critical-thinking, problem-solving, and math skills; creativity; communication skills

Certification and Licensing
Optional

Working Conditions
Indoors in office settings

Salary Range
About $53,110 to $172,010

Number of Jobs
About 1,930,300

Future Job Outlook
Growth ranges between 5 percent and 30 percent, depending on specialty

help design the computer systems that are integrated into vehicles, medical equipment, and even toys and games. Still others work in product testing. Darcy Grinold, a hardware reliability engineer at Google, tests the physical products that other engineers at Google create. In a 2017 YouTube video titled *Meet Hardware Engineers at Google*, she explains, "In my role there are three parts. Figure out how a user will use a product. Create a test that will simulate that user's use. Figure out what happened when a product breaks in that test scenario." Hardware engineers like Grinold usually have a degree in computer engineering or computer science and some knowledge of software development.

Software engineers (also known as software developers or software architects) design different types of computer software, from mobile applications and games to web browsers, databases, and operating systems. They start by analyzing what the software needs to do and then design its functionality step-by-step, using models and diagrams. Although they have extensive knowledge of computer programming, they usually do not program the software themselves (computer programmers write the software's code). They work in teams and must carefully coordinate with other team members so that all aspects of the software work together. They often have a degree in software engineering, computer science, or a related field. Software engineers who specialize in applications are known as application software engineers, while those who build operating systems are known as systems software engineers.

Software engineers can work on a wide variety of projects throughout their careers. For instance, software engineer Victoria Sun currently builds websites for a technology company but she can easily change her focus. In a 2015 YouTube video titled "Day in the Life: Software Engineer," she describes the importance of being versatile and adaptable: "Because I know how to build software, one day I can change my mind and build games, I can build an iOS app, I can build something for your phone. . . . [In this career,] there's so many different kinds of possibilities."

Systems analysts (also known as engineering systems analysts) design large computer systems to meet the needs of a business or organization. They evaluate an organization's existing technology and reorganize or redesign it to better fit their needs, integrating new technology as required. They are experts in understanding the big picture and solving big problems quickly and efficiently. They usually have a strong background in computer engineering or software development and an excellent understanding of how computer systems work together. They also understand business practices and how to optimize business performance with technology. Systems analysts have ultimate control over the computer systems within their organizations. As one systems analyst told the *Princeton Review* in a 2017 article about computer engineer/systems analyst careers, building an organization's computer systems is "like having the most expensive Tinkertoy set in the world—I love it!"

How Do You Become an IT Engineer?

Education

Although computer engineering was once a field that frequently hired people who were self-taught, more and more companies are requiring that new hires have a bachelor's degree. In general, there are five major areas of study in computer science: computer engineering, software engineering, computer science, information systems, and information technology. The first three (computer engineering, software engineering, and computer science) give students a strong background in science and engineering and prepare IT engineers for their chosen career specialties. The fourth, information systems, is a business-related degree that is an option for systems analysts. The fifth, information technology, prepares students for nonengineering roles in IT.

In general, students interested in hardware engineering usually pursue a degree in computer engineering or computer science, though some choose to major in electrical engineering or another branch of engineering. Those interested in developing software applications choose software engineering or computer science. Future systems analysts often pursue a degree in computer science or information systems. Because systems analysts need a background in business, those who have an undergraduate degree in computer science sometimes go on to get a master of business administration degree with a concentration in information systems.

Certification and Licensing

There are hundreds of different types of certifications available in the IT field. Once IT engineering students decide on their area of specialty, they can investigate what types of certifications would be most beneficial.

Students who want to become a licensed professional engineer (PE) after graduation will need to have completed an engineering or computer science program that is accredited by the Accreditation Board for Engineering and Technology. A PE license is not a requirement, but it can improve job prospects or help with advancement. License candidates must have acquired four years of related work experience after graduation and pass a two-part exam.

Volunteer Work and Internships

There are not many formal volunteer positions available in IT, though young people often gain experience by volunteering to create a website for a local nonprofit group, for instance, or volunteering to help a small business create a database. On the other hand, internships are very common in IT engineering. Many technology companies have summer internships available to high school students, and most college programs link students with companies that offer formal internships—sometimes for college credit. Internships are invaluable in the IT field—they give students real-world experience, help them network with IT professionals, and often lead to a first job after graduation.

Skills and Personality

All IT engineers must have strong critical-thinking and problem-solving skills. Creativity is also key: Engineers must often "think outside the box" when coming up with solutions to problems. Finally, IT engineers work on teams and therefore must have good communication skills and the ability to get along with others.

Systems analysts in particular must also have strong interpersonal skills and the ability to communicate with people who do not have an IT background. They must understand the needs of all of the departments within their company in order to design successful systems. They also frequently work with outside contractors, and they sometimes supervise IT staff, so they must be able to work with a wide variety of people.

On the Job

Employers

IT is used in almost every sector of the economy, and IT engineers are employed by a wide variety of industries. About one-quarter to one-third of all IT engineers are employed by technology companies, including organizations that design computer systems and software for other companies. Hardware engineers also work for manufacturing companies or companies that research and develop new technologies. Systems analysts can work in any industry that relies on large computer systems to do its day-to-day business, such as the finance and insurance industries.

Working Conditions

Most IT engineers work in an office-style environment. Hardware engineers will often spend part of their time in a research lab, where they design computer devices and may test and modify them after a prototype is made.

IT engineers work full-time. Some work more than forty hours a week, especially if they need to meet a project deadline.

Earnings

According to the Bureau of Labor Statistics (BLS), of all IT engineers, hardware engineers make the highest average salary, followed by software engineers and, finally, systems analysts. In 2016 the median annual wage for hardware engineers was $115,080, with the lowest-paid 10 percent earning about $66,870 and the highest-paid 10 percent earning about $172,010. The median annual wage for software engineers was $100,080, with the lowest-paid 10 percent earning about $53,300 and the high-

An IT engineer works on project. The three main types of IT engineers are hardware engineers, who design physical devices and their parts; software engineers, who design the computer code that operates those devices; and systems analysts, who design comprehensive computer systems.

est-paid 10 percent earning about $157,590. The median annual wage for systems analysts was $87,220, with the lowest-paid 10 percent earning about $53,110 and the highest-paid 10 percent earning about $137,690.

Opportunities for Advancement

IT engineers are often promoted to project management positions, in which they direct large hardware, software, or systems development projects. Engineers who wish to advance must keep their skills current and stay abreast of the latest technology trends. Continuing education is key for success in this field.

IT engineers who wish to advance their careers but are not interested in management often go into sales engineering or consulting. These fields generally pay more and offer more autonomy and flexibility.

What Is the Future Outlook for IT Engineers?

The BLS projects 5 percent growth in job opportunities for hardware engineers through 2026, about average. At present, there is more technological innovation in software than in hardware. However, as more and more devices use computer technology to function (such as household appliances and medical devices), more hardware engineers will be needed, especially in research and development efforts. Systems analysts will also see average growth of about 9 percent through 2026 as more industries increase their reliance on computer systems. Systems analysts who can design systems using cloud technology will be in particular demand, as will those who can meet the needs of health care providers, who are increasing their reliance on electronic health records and other forms of health care IT.

Software engineers will experience the most job growth, with a projected 24 percent increase through 2026, much faster than average for all occupations. Opportunities for applications developers will increase by 30 percent, while opportunities for systems developers will increase by 11 percent. Innovative software will be needed in the health care and medical insurance industries, and there will be an increased demand for applications on mobile devices. In addition, security threats have caused an increase in demand for security software.

Regardless of the college major they choose, students pursuing IT engineering will have a bright future. The most successful will specialize in the aspects of IT that they enjoy the most and seek out a job that allows them to practice their specialty every day.

Find Out More

Association of Software Professionals (ASP)
website: www.asp-software.org

ASP is a professional trade association for software developers. Its website includes news and articles about software development as well as discussion forums.

ComputerScience.org
website: www.computerscience.org

ComputerScience.org is a website devoted to providing trustworthy, comprehensive online resources about the field of computer science and engineering. It has information about how to become a computer engineer, information about degree programs and scholarships, and interviews with computer professionals.

Institute of Electrical and Electronics Engineers (IEEE) Computer Society
2001 L St. NW
Washington, DC 20036
website: www.computer.org

The IEEE Computer Society is an organization dedicated to promoting computer science and engineering. Its website contains articles, journals, and magazines of interest to students, information about student scholarships, and a career center.

National Center for Women and Information Technology (NCWIT)
University of Colorado
Campus Box 417 UCB
Boulder, CO 80309
website: www.ncwit.org

The NCWIT is a nonprofit community dedicated to increasing the participation of women in the field of computing. Its website includes a wealth of resources and tools designed to educate women and girls about their career options in computing as well as news and articles about women in IT.

Machinist

What Does a Machinist Do?

Most people become engineers because they love to make things. However, students are sometimes surprised to learn that engineers usually do not make the things they design—especially if those things are made out of metal. Because metal must be cut using specialized machinery, precision metal parts are usually created in a machine shop, where a machinist fabricates the object to the engineer's precise specifications. In other words, engineers design, while machinists create.

Machinists are experts in using powerful and precise machinery to cut and shape metal (and sometimes other materials like wood or plastic). They fabricate items such as engine parts, machinery parts, specialty tools, custom metal furnishings or home decor, and prototypes of new products. Some work for the aerospace industry, creating parts used in airplanes, while others work in health care, creating surgical instruments or prosthetics. In short, if an object is made out of metal, a machinist can make it.

Precision machining is a skilled trade, and machinists spend years honing their skill set. They understand the properties of metals and

At a Glance

Machinist

Minimum Educational Requirements
High school diploma or equivalent

Personal Qualities
Mechanical aptitude; computer and math skills; manual dexterity; good hand-eye coordination

Certification and Licensing
Optional

Working Conditions
Machine shop

Salary Range
About $25,900 to $62,590

Number of Jobs
About 396,200

Future Job Outlook
Growth of 2 percent

how they behave under stress, and they are highly skilled in the use of a wide variety of complex tools, from handheld metal grinders to automated cutting machines like mills and lathes. Their job is to use this expertise to figure out the best way to fabricate an object to an engineer's (or other designer's) specifications. Because machine parts often have to fit together exactly, machinists have to be extremely precise in their work. In fact, it is not unusual for machinists to make sure an object is within one one-thousandth of an inch of the design's specifications.

Many experienced machinists can design as well as fabricate objects. These people are sometimes known as engineering machinists. Some have degrees in mechanical or industrial engineering (and are sometimes known as machining engineers), while others have learned the principles of engineering on the job. Engineering machinists work with clients to design products using engineering design programs called computer-aided design (CAD) software. CAD software creates a digital 3-D design that acts as a production blueprint. The design can then be input into a computer numerically controlled (CNC) machine (an automated tool) for production.

Some engineering machinists create and sell their own designs. For instance, David Wilcox, an engineering machinist who specializes in high-performance racing engines, had an idea of how to make his clients' race cars faster. Using CAD software, he redesigned an engine cylinder head so that air flowed through it more efficiently, which made the engine more powerful. Then he used a CNC milling machine to cut the cylinder head out of a solid piece of aluminum. Engineering machinists like Wilcox often have their own machine shops and run their own businesses. "Having your own machine shop means that you can fabricate your own designs and modify them on the fly," he said to the author in a personal communication. "It's a big investment, but it can really pay off."

Precision machining is a great career choice for students who love to work with their hands and are interested in the fabrication side of engineering. It is also a good way for young people who do not plan to go to college to earn a good wage in an engineering-related field right after high school.

How Do You Become a Machinist?

Education

Precision machining is one of the few careers that young people can enter with no previous experience or training. It is more common, however, for prospective machinists to attend a one- or two-year training program at a technical school or community college. These programs teach students how to operate CNC machines and use CAD software—skills that are crucial for a successful career in a modern machine shop (and that can be hard to learn on the job). Students who have completed a training program usually have better job prospects than those who have not.

The most successful machinists have a four-year degree in mechanical engineering or a related field. A four-year degree is often a requirement for work in one of the advanced manufacturing industries, such as the aerospace industry. It is important to note, however, that mechanical engineering programs do not train students in machining. For this reason, many machinist engineers pursue their degree after working for a while as a machinist, or they learn the trade later in their engineering career.

Certification and Licensing

Machinists are not required to be certified, but certification can make it easier to get a job or an increase in pay. Various types of certification are available through the National Institute for Metalworking Skills (NIMS). NIMS offers machining certifications in about twenty areas, including CNC operation, CNC programming and setup, manual skills such as grinding and drill press operation, and job planning.

NIMS also awards national accreditation to education and training programs. Many accredited training programs—and even some more formal apprenticeship programs—prepare students to take some NIMS certification exams, so it is a good idea to choose a training program that has been accredited by NIMS.

Volunteer Work and Internships

In this field, internships are known as apprenticeships. Apprenticeships are a formalized way for a person to learn on the job. Apprenticeships are common in machining and typically last two years. Some prospective machinists start an apprenticeship after completing a training program, but others are hired as apprentices right out of high school. CNC machine operator Chris Matayer chose to enter the field in this way. As he recounted in a June 2017 post in the machinist blog *In the Loupe*, "I didn't know anything about machining when I started, but I trained side by side with other employees. I am a hands-on learner, so it was a perfect learning experience for me."

Young people with the best chances of being hired as apprentices will have a facility for math and will have taken geometry and trigonometry. Experience in metalworking or creating technical drawings (known as drafting) is also desirable. Some high schools have vocational-technical training programs that give students this experience.

Skills and Personality

Machinists must have an aptitude for using mechanical principles to solve problems. They understand the principles of engineering, have advanced skills in physics and math, and can visualize spatial relationships and understand technical drawings and models. They also must have computer skills to be able to work with CNC and CAD technology and computerized measuring machines. Finally, machinists must have good vision, hand-eye coordination, and manual dexterity, especially when doing manual work like grinding or welding.

People who are drawn to this field tend to get great satisfaction from figuring out the most efficient and practical way to get the job done. "I love figuring out how to automate things," said machinist Todd Wittac in a personal communication with the author. "One of the cool things about being a machinist is that you can use machines to build new machines." Machinists like Wittac also like working with their hands, and they enjoy the precise and exacting nature of their work.

On the Job

Employers

Most machinists are employed by machine shops, machinery manufacturing plants, or transportation equipment manufacturing plants (manufacturing plants that make vehicle parts). They can also be employed by companies or organizations that develop new technology. For instance, the National Aeronautics and Space Administration (NASA) has a dedicated machine shop that produces one-of-a-kind machined parts to modify aircraft and

Using a grinder, a machinist fabricates a part to an engineer's specifications. Machinists cut and shape metal, and sometimes other materials, to craft engine parts, machinery parts, specialty tools, custom metal furnishings or home decor, and prototypes of new products.

spacecraft or assist with research. Machinists employed by NASA produce everything from tiny micro switches to jet engine mounts to pylons that carry vehicles underneath the wings of large aircraft. NASA's machine shop also has advanced machinery, such as machines that cut metal with electric current, water, and lasers.

Working Conditions

Working in a machine shop is hazardous. Machines that cut metal create tiny chips that can enter the skin or eyes. Some machines create dust that can harm the lungs, and some are loud enough to damage hearing. The machines themselves can be dangerous as well, and accidents can cause severe injuries. In addition, machinists work with solvents and other hazardous materials. For these reasons, machinists must develop good safety habits and wear appropriate safety equipment at all times.

Machining also requires physical stamina. Most machinists must stand for most of the workday. They are often required to lift heavy objects, and they need a certain amount of physical strength to use the various tools of their profession.

Most machinists work full-time. Because most machine shops need to have their machines in operation all the time to turn a profit, machinists often do shift work, working nights or on weekends.

Earnings

According to the Bureau of Labor Statistics (BLS), the median salary for machinists was $41,700 as of May 2016, with the lowest-paid 10 percent earning about $25,900 and the highest-paid 10 percent earning about $62,590. The top-paying industry for machinists overall is transportation equipment manufacturing.

Machinists with a degree in mechanical engineering make significantly more than those who have only completed a training program or apprenticeship in machining. The BLS categorizes these degreed machinists as mechanical engineers. The median salary for mechanical engineers was $84,190 as of May 2016, with the lowest-paid 10 percent earning about $54,420 and the highest-paid 10 percent earning about $131,350.

Opportunities for Advancement

A machinist's pay is tied to his or her work experience, skill set, and credentials. Machinists improve their skills throughout their careers. Some machinists advance to supervisory positions, managing the work on the shop floor and the performance of less experienced machinists and apprentices. Others move into sales positions or interact directly with customers, using their technical expertise to sell services and oversee projects. Experienced machinists with a background in business can also open their own machine shops. These may be one-person operations or large shops that employ dozens of machinists. Some machinists get a bachelor's degree in engineering and become engineering machinists.

What Is the Future Outlook for Machinists?

The BLS projects that there will only be about a 2 percent job growth for machinists through 2026. This is due to technological advances in the industry such as a heavier reliance on CNC machines, autoloaders, and high-speed machining—all of which need less supervision. However, machinists are still needed to set up, monitor, and maintain these advanced machines. Machinists who understand the latest technology will have the best job opportunities.

Even though there will be a relatively small number of new machining jobs created through 2026, there will still be plenty of opportunities for new machinists entering the workforce. This is due to changes in the population. According to the online industry magazine *American Machinist*, 70 percent of the current workforce is over age forty-five and will be retiring over the next two decades. In addition, fewer and fewer young people are entering the skilled trades. This means that young people entering this profession will have excellent job prospects for the foreseeable future.

Find Out More

American Machinist
Oswald Centre
1100 Superior Ave., 8th Floor
Cleveland, OH 44114
website: www.americanmachinist.com

American Machinist is an online magazine and resource dedicated to educating machinists about the latest updates in the field. Its website contains news and information about all aspects of machining.

Modern Machine Shop
Gardner Business Media, Inc.
6915 Valley Ave.
Cincinnati, OH 45244
website: www.mmsonline.com

Modern Machine Shop is an online resource that shares stories of real-world applications of metalworking technology. Its website contains articles and videos about tools and machines, systems and software, and techniques.

National Institute for Metalworking Skills (NIMS)
10565 Fairfax Blvd., Suite 10
Fairfax, VA 22030
website: www.nims-skills.org

NIMS is a professional organization that certifies machinists and other metalworkers and accredits training programs. Its website includes a job center as well as information on apprenticeships, certification, and industry news.

National Tooling and Machine Association (NTMA)
website: www.ntma.org

The NTMA provides online training and information in precision machining technology. Its website includes an overview of precision machining, a resource library, and a jobs board.

Sales Engineer

What Does a Sales Engineer Do?

Most engineers spend their days at computer terminals, designing computer systems or commercial buildings or the latest mobile phone. They tend to spend months on a single project, and they rarely have any involvement in the business side of their company. While many engineers enjoy this lifestyle, it is not for everyone. For those engineers who enjoy talking about technology, like variety and travel, and enjoy taking risks, there is another career path: sales engineer.

Sales engineers are salespeople who specialize in selling complex and technologically advanced products. They have the characteristics and skill sets of both engineers and sales professionals. As engineers, they have extensive knowledge of the technical aspects of the products they sell, and they understand how those products can be modified to suit the needs of their clients. As sales professionals, they are personable and persuasive, and they can clearly communicate the benefits of their products to potential customers.

For instance, when a technology company is trying to sell its

At a Glance

Sales Engineer

Minimum Educational Requirements
Bachelor's degree in engineering, or equivalent knowledge

Personal Qualities
Technical and problem-solving skills; excellent communication and interpersonal skills

Certification and Licensing
Not required

Working Conditions
Indoors; extensive travel

Salary Range
About $56,990 to $166,500

Number of Jobs
About 74,900

Future Job Outlook
Growth of 7 percent

product to a client, it will make sure sales engineers are part of the sales team. The sales engineers know the product inside and out and can talk to the client's technical staff about it in detail. Their job is to listen to the client's needs and priorities and demonstrate how the product can meet those needs. They use their engineering skills to come up with ways to customize the product to solve a client's specific problems. Finally, they create written proposals that outline the technical aspects of the sale, describing exactly what their company will deliver to the client. Occasionally, sales engineers continue their relationships with their clients after the sale, acting as a liaison between their company and the client and troubleshooting any problems that come up.

Sales engineering is an ideal career for people who love engineering but who also enjoy meeting people, traveling, public speaking, and the art of selling. Thomas Ott, a sales engineer at a high-tech start-up company, described his job as a perfect fit for him, "[It is] a Goldilocks world of solving problems and selling the solution." As he wrote in February 2016 post on the blog *Neural Market Trends*, "Coming from the engineering world, solving problems is in my blood. Couple this with learned public speaking skills (i.e., Toastmasters), making presentations in a Sales environment makes me happy. I'm in my sweet spot."

No two days in the life of a sales engineer are the same. Ott goes on to describe what he does each day as a sales engineer:

What's my typical day like? Hectic! Unpredictable! Cool! Most of the day I'm on discovery calls with customers discussing how our platform can help them. Next I could be making a presentation with an Account Representative to a board room. After that I could be on a WebEx [video-conference] with a customer helping them troubleshoot a process. This could, and has, happened all in one day.

Sales engineers do not only sell technology; they sell a wide range of complex products and services, including industrial machinery, airliners, architectural services, weapons systems, communications systems, and medical equipment. They can go by the title of solutions engineer, customer engineer, or technical account manager.

How Do You Become a Sales Engineer?

Education

Most sales engineers start out their careers as engineers. They usually have a bachelor's or master's degree in one of the engineering disciplines and practical experience as an engineer. However, this is not always the case. If a candidate has enough knowledge of a company's product, an engineering degree may not be necessary for a successful career as a sales engineer. According to Daryl Gerke, an experienced sales engineer, "Technical experience [is] mandatory, as without it you have no credibility with technical customers. But technical degrees, although useful, are not mandatory." As he wrote in a July 2017 article for the online magazine *In Compliance*, "I've known sales engineers without degrees (as well as those with advanced degrees) who have done very well. In sales, it's the results that count."

Even though it is possible to work as a sales engineer without an engineering degree, sales engineers must acquire their technical knowledge before entering this field. For this reason, students should either pursue a bachelor's degree in a subject related to the industry in which they want to work or gain technical experience by working in that industry for a few years.

Occasionally, sales engineers start out as salespeople—an occupation that does not require a bachelor's degree. To move into a sales engineering position, these individuals must become technical experts in their chosen industry—often through a combination of experience with the products and self-directed study.

Certification and Licensing

Sales engineers are not certified or licensed, but there are various certifications available for salespeople in general. Students should research whether specific certifications will enhance their careers. Some companies do require their sales engineers to hold an engineering license. Additional certification in engineering can help with job prospects and advancement.

Volunteer Work and Internships

Because the work of a sales engineer demands advanced engineering knowledge, there are no volunteer opportunities in this field. However, engineering students interested in this career may be able to secure an internship in a sales department that employs sales engineers.

Skills and Personality

Sales engineers must have not only technical expertise but also strong people skills. They must be friendly, enjoy interacting with engineers and other technical experts, and inspire confidence and trust. Like any salesperson, sales engineers must build strong relationships with their customers.

However, sales engineers do not necessarily have to possess the typical outgoing, extroverted personality of a salesperson. "When most people think of salespeople, they think of the used car salesman. You know, pushy, manipulative, and motivated solely by money," said Gerke.

> In my experience, this is not so with sales engineers. Almost all have a "geek streak," and love to talk about technology with their technical colleagues. . . . It is not necessary to be an extrovert. Some of the most successful sales engineers I've known were quiet introverts. Since most engineers are introverts, this is often an advantage over the more traditional extroverted sales personality.

Sales engineers must also have excellent communication skills. They must be able to communicate clearly about technical subjects, listen closely to their prospective client's needs, and ask appropriate questions. And because part of a sales engineer's job is demonstrating the product, strong presentation skills are also very important, as are good writing skills.

Finally, sales engineers must be comfortable with uncertainty. Their days are always different; they work on multiple projects at the same time and must be able to shift focus at a moment's notice. In addition, because at least a portion of their pay is based on commission, their total salary fluctuates—sometimes from paycheck to paycheck. However, most sales engineers have an entrepreneurial spirit and see working on commission as an opportunity rather than a drawback. People who are most suited for this career tend to view uncertainty as an exciting part of their job.

On the Job

Employers

Sales engineers are employed by businesses that produce complex technological or scientific products and sell them to other businesses. For instance, a sales engineer with a background in civil or structural engineering may work for a commercial construction company, while an information technology sales engineer may work for a cloud computing company. According to the Bureau of Labor Statistics (BLS), the largest employers of sales engineers in 2016 were durable goods wholesalers (companies that make long-lasting goods and sell them to other businesses), manufacturing companies, and computer system design companies.

Working Conditions

Sales engineers work in offices. However, since they sell to other business, they spend a great deal of their time traveling to those businesses to demonstrate their products. Depending on their industry, they may drive or fly, but most have to travel at least several times a month. Some sales engineers travel internationally on a regular basis.

Sales engineers often work long hours, especially when on a sales call. Most sales engineers will work as many hours as it takes to make a sale—which can mean staying up all night to finish a proposal or working on the weekend to get a product demonstration ready. Some businesses require their sales engineers to be available via cell phone at all times. As Ott said, "You're going to be busy. Prepare to take calls after hours, before hours, on a train, in an airport, etc. I joke that my life would end if I lost my mobile phone."

Earnings

According to the BLS, the median salary for sales engineers was $100,000 as of May 2016, with the lowest-paid 10 percent earning around $56,990 and the highest-paid 10 percent earning about $166,500. The top-paying industry for sales engineers overall is telecommunications and computer system design.

As a salaried employee, sales engineers do not get overtime pay. Instead, sales engineers are typically paid a base salary plus commission, or a salary plus bonus. Commissions are based on the value of sales made. Commissions are added to sales engineers' paychecks periodically, but the amount fluctuates and is tied to the amount of business they generated for the company. Bonuses are usually paid annually and are often tied to an individual's performance or to the overall performance of the company. Commissions and bonuses vary greatly from industry to industry.

Sales engineers are also reimbursed for their expenses, including travel and customer entertainment (flights, hotels, meals, and so on). Some sales engineers are given the use of a company car.

Opportunities for Advancement

Sales engineers can advance to directorial positions within their company's technical sales department. Or, if they develop a strong reputation in their industry, they may be offered financial incentives to take a position with another company.

Some sales engineers become engineering consultants, selling their engineering expertise rather than a particular product. Others may move into upper management positions within engineering or technology companies.

What Is the Future Outlook for Sales Engineers?

The BLS projects that employment of sales engineers will grow 7 percent through 2026, about as fast as average for all occupations. Growth is expected to be strongest for sales engineers with an information technology background selling computer systems and related services. According to the BLS, growth in this area will reach 20 percent through 2026. In addition, because manufacturing companies are outsourcing their sales staff, the BLS projects significant growth in positions available with independent sales agencies (agencies that sell other companies' products for them).

Individuals who can pair strong technical knowledge with effective sales skills are rare. For this reason, skilled sales engineers will always be in demand. According to Gerke, "Once you get a year or two of experience—and assuming you enjoy it—you never need to worry about a job again."

Find Out More

Manufacturers' Agents National Association (MANA)
6321 W. Dempster St., Suite 110
Morton Grove, IL 60053
website: www.manaonline.org

MANA is a professional organization for technical salespeople who represent the manufacturing industry. Its website includes an industry magazine, a podcast, a blog, and information about the industry.

Manufacturers' Representatives Educational Research Foundation (MRERF)
5460 Ward Rd., Suite 125
Arvada, CO 80002
website: https://mrerf.org

The MRERF provides education and certification for professionals in technical and manufacturing sales. Its website contains information about certification and educational materials for salespeople.

Sales Engineer
website: www.thesalesengineer.com

The Sales Engineer is an online resource dedicated to sharing best practices among sales engineers and technical salespeople. Its website includes educational materials about roles and responsibilities of sales engineers, soft skills in sales, presentations, and other sales topics.

Sales Engineer Training
website: www.salesengineertraining.com

Sales Engineer Training is a training site that offers online classes in technical sales. Its free resources section contains articles, quizzes, videos, and general information about sales engineering.

Civil Engineering Technician

What Does a Civil Engineering Technician Do?

Civil engineers plan, design, and build public infrastructure projects like highway systems, water treatment plants, bridges and tunnels, reservoirs and dams, and public buildings. These large-scale projects often need thousands of people in order to complete them. A key part of any civil engineering project includes civil engineering technicians. These professionals assist civil engineers, acting as their eyes and ears on the job site—taking measurements, running tests, collecting data, and overseeing day-to-day operations. Some of their job duties include developing plans and estimating costs, coordinating with contractors and subcontractors, making sure design specifications are being followed, preparing for regulatory inspections, and documenting day-to-day operations.

Many civil engineering technicians are involved in making sure a design element has been constructed properly and safely. For instance, Mel Wright, a civil

---

At a Glance

Civil Engineering Technician

Minimum Educational Requirements
None, but associate's degree is preferred

Personal Qualities
Critical-thinking, problem-solving, and math skills; reading, writing, and other communication skills

Certification and Licensing
Optional

Working Conditions
Indoors and outdoors in offices and at job sites

Salary Range
About $31,100 to $77,500

Number of Jobs
About 74,500

Future Job Outlook
Growth of 9 percent

---

engineering technician working on a project to build a highway overpass, is in charge of making sure the base of the overpass is stable. The overpass supports are anchored into the earth with rods that are 39 feet (12 m) long. Wright conducts what is called a soil nail test: She applies a machine to the rods that measures how securely they are embedded into the layer of sandstone below. Another one of her duties on the project is assisting with structural drafting. Under the supervision of an engineer, she uses a type of 3-D computer-aided design (CAD) software called AutoCAD to update any necessary modifications to the project's design.

Civil engineering technicians are also responsible for evaluating the field conditions of a preconstruction site. For instance, Brook Seibel, a civil engineering technician in Bismarck, North Dakota, often does surveys for the Department of Transportation. She travels around her state with a team of surveyors and technicians to identify and map the location of utility poles, culverts, and other structures. Seibel then helps turn that data into a technical report that the Department of Transportation can use when planning future highway development.

Most civil engineering technicians specialize in a particular area of civil engineering. They might focus on structural projects like buildings, dams, or offshore platforms and pipelines; transportation projects like roads and railways; environmental projects like water drainage networks or flood barriers; maritime projects like ports and harbors; or geotechnical projects like mines, earthworks, or construction foundations. Even though they tend to work on the same type of project during their careers, their jobs have a lot of variety, and they rarely do the same thing two days in a row.

Becoming a civil engineering technician is a great way for people who have decided not to pursue an engineering degree to still be a key part of large-scale engineering projects. This is an ideal job for someone who is interested in managing the daily operations of construction and enjoys being an integral part of a project's successful completion.

How Do You Become a Civil Engineering Technician?

Education

Most companies that hire civil engineering technicians prefer that they have an associate's degree from an institution that has been accredited by the Accreditation Board for Engineering and Technology (ABET). These degree programs are available at community colleges, technical institutes, and some colleges and universities. Many of these institutions also have certificate programs, which usually require less time to complete. Some companies accept a civil engineering technician certificate, while other do not require any formal training at all and instead look at previous job experience.

Training programs are not all the same. Some emphasize theory, while others give students a lot of hands-on experience. For instance, the Niagara College civil engineering technician program in Niagara, Canada, gives its students hands-on experience in skills they will use in jobs available in the community. "One of the things employers look for when hiring our students is some skills in laying out construction projects," says program coordinator Gilles Laroche in a 2017 YouTube video about the program. In the video, students use specialized equipment, including GPS technology, to lay out an incline for a highway. "We were given a set of instructions," student Chantal Goertz explains, "[and] brought that into Civil 3D [an autoCAD program]. We drew a profile, we drew our alignment, and then we took those points . . . and laid them out on the field. . . . I'm actually doing work that a surveyor would be doing."

Some training programs are also tailored to prepare students for a particular industry. Because some employers want a specific skill set in their technicians, it is a good idea for students to know in what industry they wish to work and to ask a prospective employer about which schools offer the best training. Some companies even pay for a student's training at night while he or she learns on the job during the day.

Associate degree programs also prepare students to work in careers closely related to civil engineering technology. According to the civil engineering technology web page for Tidewater Community College in Norfolk, Virginia, "An associate degree in civil engineering technology allows you to enter the workforce immediately as a civil engineering technician, construction inspector, land surveyor, construction superintendent, civil draftsman or geographic information system technician."

In addition to an associate's degree program, some colleges and universities offer a bachelor's degree in engineering technology. Graduates from these programs are called civil engineering technologists. Civil engineering technologists have more extensive technical knowledge about applied engineering and often supervise technicians.

High school students can prepare for a career as a civil engineering technician by taking chemistry, physics, geometry, and trigonometry and by gaining basic knowledge about the use of common computer programs as well as design programs.

Certification and Licensing

Civil engineering technicians do not need to be licensed or certified. However, certification is available through the National Institute for Certification in Engineering Technologies (NICET). The NICET requires that technicians pass an exam and provide letters of recommendation, evidence of work history, and other requirements. Technicians must update their certification periodically, which requires some professional development.

Volunteer Work and Internships

There are few volunteer opportunities in civil engineering. High school students may be able to find an internship assisting civil engineering technicians with their work. Some of these internships may be geared toward students who are interested in becoming civil engineers rather than technicians. However, these

A civil engineering technician assists civil engineers on a construction project. These technicians take measurements, run tests, collect data, and oversee day-to-day operations. They also help develop plans, estimate costs, and coordinate with contractors and subcontractors.

internships should give students an idea of what both engineers and engineering technicians do in their work.

Some training programs have internships or work-study programs that place students in part-time positions so they can get hands-on experience as a technician while they are in school. They partner with companies that offer on-the-job training with the expectation that the student will have a stronger chance of being hired permanently after graduation.

Skills and Personality

Civil engineering technicians need strong critical-thinking and problem-solving skills. They use math frequently for analysis, design, and troubleshooting and should have strong skills in algebra, geometry, and trigonometry. They must be good observers and have strong reading and writing skills. Finally, they must be able to manage projects and prioritize their work and the work of others in order to meet project deadlines.

On the Job

Employers

Traditionally, civil engineers work on publicly funded projects, but a civil engineering technician can translate his or her skills into both the public and private sector. According to the Bureau of Labor Statistics (BLS), 46 percent are employed by state and local governments and 42 percent by private engineering services (who often are hired to complete government projects). A small percentage work in the construction industry or for architectural firms. The US military also trains and employs civil engineering technicians, though experts note that military training of engineering technicians can be highly specialized and may not be good preparation for work in the civilian sector.

Working Conditions

Civil engineering technicians work in offices and at job sites. Some civil engineers travel from site to site and may use their car as a mobile office. They often work in teams with other technicians, surveyors, and construction workers.

Technicians usually work full-time, but their schedule can vary. Civil engineering projects are often scheduled during nights, weekends, or holidays so that they do not disrupt the public. Other projects are seasonal; for instance, many construction projects are scheduled during the summer, when there is more daylight. This can mean that civil engineering technicians work more hours in the summer months or must work nights or weekends on some projects. However, this varies from job to job, and many civil engineering technicians work regular business hours.

Earnings

The BLS reports that the median annual wage for civil engineering technicians in May 2016 was $49,980. The lowest-paid 10 percent earned about $31,100, and the highest-paid 10 percent earned around $77,500. Technicians working for local government earned the most, while those working in state government earned the least. Alaska offered the highest pay, with an average salary of $71,710, followed by the District of Columbia at $68,120. California offered the third-highest average salary of $66,230. California also employs more than ten times the number of technicians as Alaska and the District of Columbia combined.

Opportunities for Advancement

Civil engineering technicians advance by gaining experience within their specialty and by pursuing certification and professional development opportunities. Increasing their skills in reading engineering plans and in using computer programs like AutoCAD and spreadsheet programs is also helpful, as is increasing their experience with geographic information systems and Global Positioning Systems. As technicians gain more experience, they are given more responsibility over projects.

Some civil engineering technicians choose to advance by pursuing a degree in civil engineering, while others pursue a degree in civil engineering technology. There is a lot of overlap between the two fields, but in general, engineering programs focus on theory and engineering concepts to prepare civil engineers to be designers. Engineering technology programs prepare civil engineering technologists to execute those designs, which makes them more closely related to engineering technician programs. According to the online job and recruiting website Glassdoor, in 2017 the average salary for civil engineering technologists was about $73,000.

What Is the Future Outlook for Civil Engineering Technicians?

According to the American Society of Civil Engineers, the United States needs to invest $4.5 trillion by 2025 to improve the country's roads, bridges, dams, airports, schools, and other elements of public infrastructure. More than two hundred thousand bridges are more than fifty years old, and many of the 1 million large pipes that make up the public water system have been in use for almost one hundred years. Railways, ports, public transit systems, and wastewater treatment plants all need repair to keep people safe and the economy growing. Infrastructure projects are extremely popular with the public, and recently there has been some political will to invest more in infrastructure. If that happens, civil engineering technicians should experience substantial job growth.

Currently, the BLS estimates that jobs for civil engineering technicians will grow by 9 percent through 2026, about as fast as average. The BLS projects that some new jobs will come in the renewable energy field, as more technicians will be needed to assist engineers in building wind farms or installing solar power infrastructure. However, federal leadership is no longer focused on these new industries, so it is unclear whether there will be growth in this area.

The BLS also notes that technicians will face strong competition for job openings. The best strategy for a new technician is to stay abreast of the latest engineering software developments. Civil engineering technicians who are skilled in the newest Auto-CAD and related software will be valuable to engineers who may not have been trained on these technologies.

Even though changing governmental priorities makes it difficult to accurately project the future outlook for civil engineering technicians, eventually their role will be crucial to repairing the United States' aging infrastructure. This means that increased job growth in this career is very likely.

Find Out More

American Society of Certified Engineering
Technicians (ASCET)
15621 W. Eighty-Seventh St. Pkwy. #205
Lenexa, KS 66219
website: www.ascet.org

The ASCET is the only national professional organization for engineering technicians and technologists of all disciplines. Its website lists contact information for all local and regional chapters, which can offer guidance to students interested in civil engineering technician training programs. It also has several scholarships available for students.

American Society of Civil Engineers (ASCE)
1801 Alexander Bell Dr.
Reston, VA 20191
website: www.asce.org

The ASCE is the nation's oldest engineering society, representing more than 150,000 civil engineering professionals. Its website contains information about careers in civil engineering, conferences and events, and an extensive library that includes books, a newsroom, and industry reports, including the *2017 Report Card for America's Infrastructure.*

Civil and Structural Engineer
website: https://csengineermag.com

Civil and Structural Engineer is an online magazine that provides news and information about the civil and structural engineering industry. Its website contains articles, videos, podcasts, and industry news about the civil engineering industry.

National Institute for Certification in Engineering Technologies (NICET)
1420 King St.
Alexandria, VA 22314
website: www.nicet.org

The NICET is the certifying body for engineering technicians and technologists. Its website offers information about certification requirements, lists current job openings, and contains news articles of interest to engineering technicians and technologists.

Interview with an IT Engineer

Tim D'Angelo is an information technology (IT) engineer with twenty years' combined experience in the IT and telecommunications fields. Currently, he is the technical service manager at the Federal Reserve Bank in Richmond, Virginia. D'Angelo was interviewed via e-mail about his career.

Q: Why did you become an IT engineer?
A: While I was pursuing my electrical engineering degree, I was hired by Gateway Computers as technical support in their call center. I discovered I understood technology like I was fluent in its language. Twenty-plus years ago, working in IT was not as common as it is today, so while in college I took additional technology courses at another school to try and get my foot in the door. Fate had it that when I graduated college, I ended up in telecommunications designing Dominion Energy's communications systems rather than designing network or security architecture as I had planned.

Q: Can you describe your typical workday?
A: My typical workday is rarely typical. Probably the only constant is that I attend way too many meetings to discuss the portfolio of projects I support on any given day. My day can be boring: sometimes I spend the day ensuring data is classified correctly, or compiling a presentation for executives who I hope will give me support, or creating documentation for one of my lines of business. My day can also be exciting, like if a system I am responsible for fails and if we don't fix the issue, hundreds of millions of dollars in securities cannot be purchased or transferred. These are the kinds of things that make the evening news.

Q: What do you like most about your job?

A: I enjoy the diversity of my job, as it constantly keeps me learning. I rarely get to rest—once I provide an answer or solution, my customers have moved on to wanting their products to do more or work faster or be cheaper. I also enjoy the flexibility my job allows me, as I do not always have to work from my desk if everything is running smoothly. I can work from my mobile phone or boot up the laptop and hold a conference or troubleshooting session while I'm sitting outside.

Q: What do you like least about your job?

A: Every pro has its con, so with the flexibility and diversity comes the constant change and lack of boundaries. Basically, everything my customers need funnels through me, so I'm always slightly confused and constantly seeking answers.

Q: What personal qualities do you find most valuable for this type of work?

A: Curiosity, organizational skills, and being able to work with introverted people. Curiosity is required, as IT is always changing, and if you're not passionate about learning, you can't keep up and add value to whatever you support. Organizational skills are also required—I have to be able to structure my work and manage my time because I routinely have conflicting tasks/requests/priorities. Since I can only do one thing at a time, I have to ensure I'm working on the right tasks while still tracking those items I'm not actively working on, which is why time management and documentation skills are so important. Finally, it takes a certain kind of people skills to be a manager in IT. There are great minds in this field, but sometimes these same highly intelligent people are reluctant to talk or engage. Some of these people have answers to very difficult problems, and it's my job to earn their trust and create a safe zone so they will share their ideas and take risks.

Q: What is the best way to prepare for this type of job?

A: You can't force yourself to like technology. However, if you enjoy discovering how things work, enjoy making things, and like coding or robotics or any other aspect of technology, then odds are you'll enjoy a career in IT engineering. Loving what you do aside—the best way to prepare for any career is to research those who have been successful before you and find out what made them successful. Was it [Apple founder Steve] Jobs's personality or his perseverance that made him the technology giant he was? Is it [Tesla and SpaceX founder] Elon Musk's innovation or his gift for applying technology to practical use that makes him successful? Learn from those who have walked the path before you and work on adapting their strengths into your core strengths.

Q: What other advice do you have for students who might be interested in this career?
A: This job is not about instant gratification. It's not like the movies; we aren't pulling laptops out of our backpacks and hacking into ATM machines or the NSA [National Security Agency] in a matter of seconds. Solving problems as an IT engineer in a large shop can feel like trying to turn a battleship with one canoe paddle: you'll get there with enough effort and patience, but it won't be quick.

Other Jobs in Engineering

Aerospace engineer
Agricultural engineer
Aquaculture engineer
Architect
AutoCAD designer
Automation engineer
Automotive engineer
Biological engineer
Cartographer
Chemical engineer
Civil engineer
Drafter
Drafting and design engineer
Electrical engineer
Electromechanical technician

Fire protection engineer
Geological engineer
Industrial engineer
Landscape architect
Marine engineer
Materials engineer
Mechanical engineer
Mining engineer
Naval architect
Nuclear engineer
Nuclear safety engineer
Photogrammetrist
Structural engineer
Surveyor
Tool and die maker

Editor's note: The US Department of Labor's Bureau of Labor Statistics provides information about hundreds of occupations. The agency's *Occupational Outlook Handbook* describes what these jobs entail, the work environment, education and skill requirements, pay, future outlook, and more. The *Occupational Outlook Handbook* may be accessed online at www.bls.gov/ooh.

Index